THE PORTAGE POETRY SERIES

SERIES TITLES

A Bright Wound
Sarah A. Etlinger

The Velvet Book
Rae Gouirand

Table with Burning Candle
Julia Paul

Listening to Mars
Sally Ashton

Glitter City
Bonnie Jill Emanuel

The Trouble with Being a Childless Only Child
Michelle Meyer

Happy Everything
Caitlin Cowan

Dear Lo
Brady Bove

Sadness of the Apex Predator
Dion O'Reilly

Do Not Feed the Animal
Hikari Miya

The Watching Sky
Judy Brackett Crowe

Let It Be Told in a Single Breath
Russell Thorburn

The Blue Divide
Linda Nemec Foster

Lake, River, Mountain
Mark B. Hamilton

Talking Diamonds
Linda Nemec Foster

Poetic People Power
Tara Bracco (ed.)

The Green Vault Heist
David Salner

There is a Corner of Someplace Else
Camden Michael Jones

Everything Waits
Jonathan Graham

We Are Reckless
Christy Prahl

Always a Body
Molly Fuller

Bowed As If Laden With Snow
Megan Wildhood

Silent Letter
Gail Hanlon

New Wilderness
Jenifer DeBellis

Fulgurite
Catherine Kyle

The Body Is Burden and Delight
Sharon White

Bone Country
Linda Nemec Foster

Not Just the Fire
R.B. Simon

Monarch
Heather Bourbeau

The Walk to Cefalù
Lynne Viti

The Found Object Imagines a Life: New and Selected Poems
Mary Catherine Harper

Naming the Ghost
Emily Hockaday

Mourning
Dokubo Melford Goodhead

Messengers of the Gods: New and Selected Poems
Kathryn Gahl

After the 8-Ball
Colleen Alles

Careful Cartography
Devon Bohm

Broken On the Wheel
Barbara Costas-Biggs

Sparks and Disperses
Cathleen Cohen

Holding My Selves Together: New and Selected Poems
Margaret Rozga

Lost and Found Departments
Heather Dubrow

Marginal Notes
Alfonso Brezmes

The Almost-Children
Cassondra Windwalker

Meditations of a Beast
Kristine Ong Muslim

PRAISE FOR

A BRIGHT WOUND

What a moving and timely book. In our world of hard lines, *A Bright Wound* celebrates tension, *betweenness*, the "foraging" for a home that transcends meanness or binaries. Etlinger faces our shared histories of violence and warns us, we're coming up short: "Survival […] just a sound a word makes." Still, these poems doggedly ask "what if?" – of the poet's own experiences, of those entrenched in their ways, even of myth. *What if?* They call out what threatens to destroy us, but somehow, light seems to be everywhere, peeking through the blinds, and rebellion rises into a real possibility. Fingers move along prayer beads. Fields, miraculously, endure. *Tikkun olam*, repairing the world, continues in its quiet work: "In darkness, light is a blessing./ Against its silhouette, almost anything is possible." As a reader, I felt both affirmed and challenged by this book, and in that way, these poems demonstrate something incredibly rare: wisdom.

—Allison Adair
author of *The Clearing*

"I come to this work honestly," Sarah A. Etlinger writes in this so fittingly titled new collection, *A Bright Wound*, and though this proclamation refers to the tough work of protection—of the self, the son, the environment—it applies to the collection as a whole. I cannot say this about every poetry collection, or every poet. For this reason, she is an apt poet-storyteller, one willing to take the risk of telling the story—of the Hanukkah Dinosaur, Winter, the High Holy Days, and my personal favorite, the prairie—not in prose but in verse.

—Jenna Goldsmith
author of *Crush*
Poet Laureate, City of Rockford, Illinois

One translation of the etymology of "midrash" is to seek with care which is how I experienced Etlinger's stunning poems in *A Bright Wound*. Through a retelling of the story of Persephone, how she left her mother and found love in the underworld, how she grew a self out of refusal and came to redeem the whole world in her act of revolt, *A Bright Wound* is a delicate and tender examination of the many conflicting facets of the self as daughter, wife, mother, and lover as well as an interrogation of family history, memory, faith, and landscape: "a swallow, a burst, the shallow opening—but a life is not a myth." In the introductory poem the speaker says "I am both the good daughter and the rebel" and the reader comes to see this split self as a blessing, like the bright wound at the center of the book, a pomegranate and six seeds, a gift of both pain and promise. The poems enquire on the meaning and paradox of cycles of time and seasons, grief and redemption, love and forgiveness through the power of language to bind and unbind, create and recreate. "Isn't that how it goes?/Doesn't everything end in words?/Not ashes to ashes, dust to dust,/but life into words./We are spun. We are storied."

—Heathen Derr-Smith
author of *Thrust*

A
BRIGHT
WOUND

SARAH A. ETLINGER

CORNERSTONE PRESS
UNIVERSITY OF WISCONSIN-STEVENS POINT

Cornerstone Press, Stevens Point, Wisconsin 54481
Copyright © 2024 Sarah A. Etlinger
www.uwsp.edu/cornerstone

Printed in the United States of America by
Point Print and Design Studio, Stevens Point, Wisconsin

Library of Congress Control Number: 2024935378
ISBN: 978-1-960329-36-3

Cornerstone Press titles are produced in courses and internships offered by the
Department of English at the University of Wisconsin–Stevens Point.

DIRECTOR & PUBLISHER
Dr. Ross K. Tangedal

EXECUTIVE EDITORS
Jeff Snowbarger, Freesia McKee

EDITORIAL DIRECTOR
Ellie Atkinson

SENIOR EDITORS
Brett Hill, Grace Dahl

PRESS STAFF
Carolyn Czerwinski, Sophie McPherson, Eva Nielsen, Natalie Reiter, Ava Willett

In loving memory of Kelly Baran, 1983–2023.
This book is for you.

ALSO BY SARAH A. ETLINGER:

The Weather Gods
Little Human Things
Never One for Promises

CONTENTS

The Winter Seeds   1

WINTER

Hanukkah Dinosaur   4

How to Survive the Winter   6

Hades to Persephone, the First Night   7

Clothesline   8

Persephone, the Morning After   9

Demeter Unbound, Winter   10

If He Had Offered Her His Heart   11

SPRING

Persephone on Grief   14

Givens   15

The Trial   16

Polaris   19

Letter to Persephone, Before Mother's Day   20

In Which I Try to Forgive You   21

Persephone's Lament, Early Spring   22

Magnolia   23

The Ducks   24

Now That It's Over I Think I Love You More   25

Lost Cause   26

A BRIGHT WOUND

Pomegranate–Calyx–An Essay   28

Day of Reckoning   30

Demeter's Regrets   34

To the Neighbor's Young Daughter Who Is   35
  Learning to Be Brave

Five Simple Dots of Light   36

In the Red Room   38

Self-Portrait as Persephone   39

Poem with an Elephant   40

Girl Talk   41

Sometimes Demeter Wishes   42

Blackbird, Butterfly, Robin   43

Sometimes Love Looks Just like a Field   44

Self-Portrait Where my Mother is a Nun   45
  and I'm A Good Daughter

The Rabbit   47

Paradise   48

SUMMER

In the Kingdom of Light   50

Persephone, Her First Summer Back Home   53

The Thing You Thought You Wanted   54

The Deepest Images of Our Universe   55
  are Here on Earth

In the Watermelon Fields of Kansas   56

Poem with Husband and Turtle   57

The Thought of You Singing   58

Hades Advises Demeter   59

Persephone to Hades, Late August   60

2300 Friday Nights   61

Hades, Summer Solstice   62
After Death   63
The Field   64
Daily Work   66
Love is an Intransitive Verb   67
Stocking the Lagoon   68
Dream (Persephone)   69
Entering the World Again   70
Parachuters   71

FALL

Tether   74
Persephone on Fate   75
After Demeter's Therapist tells her to find 5 things   77
    she can see to cope with her grief
Erev Rosh Hashanah   78
All Hallows   79
God Loves You '22   80
Conchology   82
Etrog   83
Farginen   84
Yom Kippur   85
Ritual   86
An Old White Door   87
pomegranate/seeded apple/beginnings   89

Notes   91
Acknowledgments   93

The Winter Seeds

As with most things, there are two versions:
in one version of the myth, the daughter is abducted and tricked
into staying by eating pomegranate seeds. The mother mourns,
and with her, the earth grows barren;
only when reunited with her daughter does it bloom again.

In the other version, the rebellious daughter
chooses the world of the dead to help quiet
their souls. Yet, the mother's grief
is the same, though she is absent in this story.

    I am both the good daughter and the rebel.
    I am the familiar and the stranger.
    I am the desire for connection and the thrill
    of severance: I have cut that which ties together
    and I have connected what has loosed.

    What is bound can be unbound:
    ties that bind can also unbind.
    My mother's words ring like empty houses:
    You do or you don't.
    At her root there is nothing
    or anything. Something might well be nothing if
    it's not what you want, if
    it's not what you need.

    You can't be both dead and alive.
    And yet there is always a desire for more:
    for something beyond the body.

Consider: to have a body is to contend with violence.
Not the everyday violence of bruises and scrapes,
the usual injury of use. But the violence of knowledge.
The fact of death.
At birth our bodies enter life already reaching toward death.
                At birth we are victims of this violence.

Consider: to swallow and chew is to mutilate.
To open a pomegranate is to bear witness to a wound,
to seeds that look like blood.
To cut to the core is an act of violence—
yet the seeds also bear witness.

> To be fertile is to store within our cells the fact of birth
> which is also a death which is also an act of violence.
> Violence—on the body. On the heart. On time.

Maybe the prize of immortality is to finally be free from violence.

Maybe the reason Persephone ate those seeds—those winter seeds—
the seeds that devastated her mother
was that she found a way to be both dead and alive;
to have a body free from violence.

WINTER

Hanukkah Dinosaur

Judaism is trending again, my friend Jared tells me,
so I wonder if I should buy Dinokkah,
the inflatable Hanukkah Dinosaur,
who is bright green with a blue T-shirt, cartoon
menorah blazing on the front, and a big blue
dreidel lying on its side. He wears a white yarmulke,
which you can only see from the back.
Everything is lit from the bottom.

Imagine, I respond, *you too
can have a Hanukkah dinosaur in your front window or yard.*

I want him the way adults want things
to remind themselves they were once children.
I do not buy him.

Lately people are asking me
if I've noticed how anti-Semitism is getting worse
or if I think people aren't afraid of anything anymore.

Bob asks me quietly, and is very concerned.
Last week I told him *do not read any of the tweets
or the headline in the NYT calling a blatant attack on Jews
purported anti-semitism*—instead of what it actually was,
actual anti-semitism. *Do not,* I said, *think harder about
the Jewish Space Lasers or the LA bridge protesters
or Adidas.*

Another friend texts me about Kanye West
and says *he's a fucking asshole looking for more power,*
and I say *Yeah, but we took down our mezuzah this week
for the first time ever.* She is silent for several minutes
before she tells me about the football game. She doesn't know
what to do or say about any of this.
They all want something different
for me, and when someone asks what they can do,

I want to tell them to buy this dinosaur,
so I can rig him up on my small unruly yard
for everyone to see as they pass by, on their way to elsewhere,
as they whiz past warm glowing plastic faces
of the tiny wan Jesus and Mary and Joseph, dingy lambs
weary at the end of the shepherd's crook, the molded
shepherd's face hidden by his modest plastic cloak—

the dinosaur bright and garishly green, proud and smiling
instead of somber—a wholly joyful amalgam:

two ancient entities older than all this grass and pavement
and even this darkening sky, its hollow core
full of air and light quietly humming.

How to Survive the Winter

Gather all the light you can hold.
In a tall glass, drink it down,
each dissolved marble coating your throat.

Don't build a fire. Become one:
proud and long and determined.
Harvest the blue tongue from the flames.

At dusk, follow the light to where it opens,
and then unroll your voice.

Wait for morning, when the clouds form
a lush green prairie of desire.

Whether the river's long back laughs
straight into spring or it must coil
and stretch around ice, remember:

survival is just a sound a word makes.

Winter and summer will come
whether we're here, or whether we say
this word, or *this* word, or *this* one.

Hades to Persephone, the First Night

You see nothing but darkness here.

What is light but the underside of darkness?

Call it what you want: a haunting. Détente:

the trees against a brackish moon,

the rigid line of the sea hunkered down for its brooding sleep,

the song when the wind draughts autumn, a wail in the night-charred sky.

What sails us dreamward sends us back to our shallow grave—

a wing cut from airless flight,

black branches still clawing at the moon.

Clothesline

Twice now I have mistaken the winter light for sun.
Instead, thin shadows sigh

still as glass and silent
across the gentle clothesline of snow.

Sleeping branches stretch fingers into the cold
and pull my dingy memory out to wash and drape.

The white sheets shudder once,
then settle undisturbed, wait for evening.

Persephone, the Morning After

No birdsong or flight stains the sunrise.

The curtain remains still in the humming
quiet light from the small lamp.

Last night's garments litter the floor like deflated bodies.

Last night you and I leapt from one
form to another, in and out
of each other's skins. I wore
your sleeve of scars
before our long sleep.

This morning, in the mirror, I slip last night's wisp
of a robe over my arms
and seem to burnish with a different light.

Demeter Unbound, Winter

Some say winter is born wet and wild,
screaming in the night.

I don't mind the noise.
I prefer the cold when it sneaks up on me.
What keeps us bodied keeps us warm.

Over there are the remains
of the wooden altar
where I prayed, day and night,
for your return.

A chipmunk dives over the bruise
on the earth where it stood
and darts back into evening's final gesture
before dark.

Let winter run roughshod through the ripples in my hair.
Let the cold bless my ragged knees.
Let the wind shriek and scream.

Stay as long as you like.

I have been here before; I have no fear.

If He Had Offered Her His Heart

What if, instead of a pomegranate,
Hades had offered Persephone
his heart,
and she took it,
believing we would understand
the symbol,

and she took it,
knowing we who came after
would not mistake it
for a simple fruit,

and she swallowed it,
trusting we would understand

how such a small thing
can become your only sustenance?

SPRING

Persephone on Grief

Now when I think of crocuses
I think of the death of winter—
all its whitewashed light dies
and no one mourns.

Now when I watch his hands
and their measured turn toward Death,
how he balances it so carefully,

I remember to hold steady
all things that would unravel me.

Givens

The pair of house finches arrives again,
singing, topping the spruce which nudges

into the swathes of a faded spring sky.
Spring breaks—a given, heavy thing,

like the leaden blue of the ocean.
These colors, this wind, this song—none of it keeps.

Nor do the stars ever stretch
beyond their light.

The Trial

My friend Kevin and I are talking about forgiveness.

We're sitting in a diner, one of those chrome
and red ones that wants to bring us
back to the past while reminding us
we're still human, that we still crave
greasy French fries and the relief
of chalky milkshakes.

On the screen behind us,
the news story breaks about the murder trial.
That guy should rot in hell, I say.
Kevin takes a French fry off my plate and asks,
So that's it? That's what we should do?

It was clear, I say. There was definite evidence.
He confessed. That's it. Fifteen to life.
He won't get out even on parole.
Actions have consequences.
You break the law, you go to jail.

No, he says. That's not what I mean.
He looks over the rim of the red frosted plastic cup.
What if you were judged by the worst thing you ever did,
on the worst day of your life?

What kind of question is that? I say.
I wouldn't kill someone.

Maybe you might, he says, leaning back
against the leather of the booth.
You might, if your life or the life of someone you love is in danger.

That's self-defense. That's different, I protest.

He pulls out his wallet to leave bills on the table.
Remember when you told me how,
when you left your grandfather's wake,
everyone was upset you were going back to work?
Yes, I say, sucking the last morsels of milkshake
from the straw so loudly the waitress looks over.

So what?

You said, My staying won't bring him back.

It wouldn't. He died. We were sad. I could be sad
at home, or at work. It didn't matter if I sat there
in that house for a year. What good would it do?

Right, he agrees. Putting this man in jail
won't bring his girlfriend back.

But it will give the family some closure or peace.
The knowledge that justice was done, I say.

By now, people gather at the door,
waiting for our table. We get our jackets,
count some change, leave it in a pile.
As I stand up, I sling my coat across my shoulders,
catch the television screen again.

The victim's family—two parents, a small child—
are holding hands. The murderer's mother is there, too,
and leans in to the microphone,
wavers, and then says, "I know what it's like
to lose a child. I know what it's like
to feel lost. I am deeply sorry
that my loss has birthed another."

We leave the diner for the busy afternoon.
The leaves have just started to emerge

from the tips of branches. The light is still pale—
waterlogged and unsure. We pass an old building
with a man, homeless, out in front, holding out a cup.
I place the remainder of my change in it,
take the bus home.

Polaris

The ancient oak had been cut down—
its rotten core now visible like an open mouth.
In the mellow light it seemed almost peaceful,
like Ingres' Odalisques:
graceful, arms above head, shoulders bare, reposing
as if preparing for a long bath.

The trunk, scarred from the chainsaw's thin,
even slices, knew what the bare branches—
still reaching skyward—ignored:
the tapered red buds raw in their newness
will never open to leaves.

Often the body knows
what the mind cannot accept.

When night unfolds its hand to reveal the stars,
the first to appear is Polaris, pouring down its dead light
over this tree, this slope and the still, dark palm
of lagoon full now of ducks and geese
returned to spring nesting grounds.

Blackbirds perch now in the dried reeds,
their cracked raspy voices calling, calling.

Letter to Persephone, Before Mother's Day

(after Erika Meitner's "Letter on Gratitude")

Dear Persephone, today I stood in line at the post office to buy stamps so I could mail my Mother's Day cards & I wondered, *What would a Mother's Day card from Hell look like?*

These cards have flowers & rhinestones, filigree butterflies & bright-colored calligraphed expressions of gratitude as if fuchsia envelopes & happy birds can make anything about motherhood easier. The moment I affix the stamps & slide the cards into the mail slot

they are wheeling my mother into surgery for her hysterectomy, removing my place of origin—all the cells that were in my mother & grandmother before I was an I, before my mother was an I, before my grandmother even knew there was a thing called love. I confess I don't know how

to feel about it. Sometimes when I talk about love I am really thinking about death. I should feel like an orphan, but I don't. I told a friend I thought you were brave, that I want to be like you.

You have taken what you were given—desiccated seeds—& grew them into a kingdom & you blessed them without your mother's blessing, knowing she was somewhere, still angry. Sometimes I feel like a gull soaring above the grocery store parking lot searching

for any scrap to make a home, a life foraged from shards & ribbon. We can all make something from nothing, like you. We can all sing. I want to know my mother is there without having to feel her sadness. Can we ever get away from feeling another's sadness?

I should feel homeless, yet I don't. Except my body won't stop swaying as if it were a boat let loose on open water near a dusky horizon.

In Which I Try to Forgive You

It was an unsaid thing, a covenant—
a promise made as the sun burned in,
quiet as snow.

Yet what is a promise but an acknowledgment
that something might otherwise end?

Look at the way the early light
rustles the water, its stillness a song.

Look at the African violet we planted
because your mother grew them,
brooding in the window.

We called that a promise,
an opportunity to make things better.

The cardinal, singing but invisible,
calls it business as usual.

Its throbs of sound
fade like clouds, leaving
no evidence except memory
for those who stopped to witness
its brevity.

Say you create something beautiful.
It enters the world raw and wet,
on unsteady legs.
It grows into its own life,
and then it ends.

Maybe what my friend Molly says is true:
forgiveness isn't
for the other person.
It's for you.

Persephone's Lament, Early Spring

I cannot think with all this color
burning around me.

A pyre of yellow forsythia
swallows its branches.

Scarlet tulips flame out of the earth,
and amber carp swim

under the black water
like sparks under a kettle.

The rosy magnolia still smolders
after the morning's bleach fog dissipates.

Even in the narrow bands of blue
before the moon ignites,

the heavy gray of smoke
burns my nose.

I open the window
to let the air in.

It is not color I hate, but its dying.

Magnolia

The last remnant of winter,
a waterlogged half-moon waning
already at dawn,
waits to pass through
the sun's yellow door,
where the final shred
of winter's promise fades.

There's a reason April is cruel:
the cones from the lone red pine
now skirt the earth and brood;
within the bulbs and seeds
reside the roots of their own undoing.

Yet who can resist April's shine,
heavy in the air like magnolia,
in the morning, breathing in
all this life?

The Ducks

Every so often one of us will write the other, *I miss the ducks.*
Then time opens and it's as if we are back there again
in the grubby plastic chairs you'd salvaged. The afternoon light
glimmered to halo us. We might have been angels.

The mallards would huddle, wander about,
chatter, then disappear to the edge
of the pond just out of sight.

Every so often things return and go and return:
the ducks back from their winter flight somehow
older and less downy, quieter. Us in those chairs,
and the chickens, and the rabbits,
before the coyotes got them—
and with those ducks.

Now That It's Over I Think I Love You More

It's when I've set myself to something else:
grocery lists, laundry, appointments,
scribbling mindless as the moon—
that's when I think of all that I want to show you.

The new cactus. How it seems to take well
to the light in the bay window and how every day
its long finger points in all directions
as if to say *Look around you. Look at everything.*

How the grackles swarm the field,
convening in their frenetic brevity.

How the morning light turns into a waiting,
crowned atop a tree or a single bead across the water.

How yesterday the spruce finally came down,
and how in all the new light, the world was blue
and bright again.

How this life is green and full of shells.

Look. Look at everything.

How shadows on the sidewalks lengthen and thin
into the shapes our bodies make as we move.

How we give.

How forgiveness is harder.

How it leaves things behind
and doesn't look back.

Lost Cause

Cut down one tree and replace it with a wishing well
deep as the night and dark as a raven's love.

Count how many birds you find,
in the city or elsewhere.

Write the number on your palm
or on old socks, or at the bottom of a glass

and tell your husband,
your lover,
a wayward lonely ant,
a stray dog—

Today I saw 23 birds.
Did you know?
Not a single one
was alone.

A BRIGHT WOUND

Pomegranate—Calyx—an Essay

The pomegranate is unique in that it has what is called a persistent calyx which remains after the flowers wither and contains the ovary. The calyx, then, protects the fruit and seeds, and aids in pollination.

Such a fact is not lost on me.

I spend my life trying to protect things: myself from the ravages of anxiety; my son from whatever in this world bites and claws and depletes, from cold and too much heat and excess; the birds in the backyard from hunger and illness. I will spend hours scouring the ground for bits and pieces of plastic, fragments that could choke, litter that becomes a hazard for anyone or anything slipping by.

I come to this work honestly. My mother, too, spends her time this way: her remedy for anything is to flush the body with water to drive out disease, to purify, to nourish, refresh, energize.

And in theory this works. Water cleans; it is a baptism even if you (like me) don't believe in God. Water purifies, even if you don't deserve it.

But real life doesn't work this way. I think of Persephone, thrust into the underworld without her mother's protection. Her parched body cried for sustenance, for water. She could not partake, for she knew that if she did, she must remain there.

My mother would say that perhaps Persephone's problem in the first place was that she didn't drink enough water. Had she drunk her water, my mother's logic goes, she wouldn't have been so thirsty, and could have resisted Hades' offer of pomegranate seeds.

This is where logic and theory break down. Instead, whether by fate or rebellion, Persephone swallows the seeds. These seeds—these winter seeds—wash through her like the river Styx. She has to stay in the underworld. She becomes Queen of the Dead.

Sometimes, water hurts.

When I had mono, my mother made me drink so much water that I exhausted myself from all the trips to the bathroom.
I didn't know that I could simply refuse, the way Persephone, like most everyone else had been taught to do. *What did I fear?*
She must have been so scared—separate from her mother

for the first time, in a strange world without being able to eat or drink.

She knew she could refuse.

But her body told her differently.

Her parched body cried for sustenance. The need in her body was stronger than her mother's need to protect her.

Sometimes, daughters do what they must.

Like water, they follow the path of least resistance. They carve new paths. They squeeze between small spaces and enlarge them, or flow toward the ocean, toward limitless vastness.
What do mothers think they are protecting?

The pomegranate's persistent calyx understands what none of us did: to protect a seed, finally, is to ensure that it is safe: that it will grow into its own fruit, with its own seeds. To fully protect must be to understand that bodies must separate, have needs beyond yours; that they may refuse to take what they know has consequences, or that they will if something deep in their body desires.

Demeter's Regrets

i

That I had not been with you that day.

That when you called out for me,
I hadn't heard you.
I hadn't come.

That I had let you go in the first place,
that I'd said *stay where I can see you*,
then turned my back.

That you needed me, and I hadn't been there.
That you hadn't run off to look for me.

That I couldn't pull you from his arms,
or how, just in time, I hadn't stepped back outside
the day a strange man drove by the house
when you'd been playing alone in the yard.

I regret that the flower hadn't been ordinary
and that I had taught you to love flowers.

That I taught you their names: *Lilac.*
Rhododendron. Flowering almond. Juniper. Yew.
Lily of the valley. Forsythia. Crocus.

That I showed you where they were in the garden,
when we looked for grubs and caterpillars
hidden among the bulbs.

That I taught you to spell the names of the flowers,
to spell so early. When the aunts came
you took them outside to show them the garden.
You spelled *crocus*, your chubby finger pointing as you said each letter.

That the aunts and I had praised you,
had told that story for years every time
the crocuses came up.

That when you were two I covered
your bare feet in dirt and wished
I could plant them, to grow
another one of you:
that I took a picture.

(You wore that sweet lavender dress—
your dark hair just beginning to curl.
I tied it with a ribbon to match
the crocus shade of your skirt.
I gave you a tulip).

That I had given you a crown of pansies
to wear for your sixth birthday.
That at night I removed it while you slept,
dried it on pieces of satin ribbon, hanging it from your window.
See? It seemed to say. This is spring, even in winter.

ii

I regret that I cut
your fruit so carefully, held it in my palms.
You would take its sweetness so readily. You trusted.
That when there were seeds, I said, *look at them. Take them*
in your mouth and place them on your tongue. Feel their shape.
Then spit them in your hand. This is life, where all life begins.

That I taught you to sing.
and that even the shape of the winter sun is a lyric,
like a life unfolding.

I regret that when you found
a trinket or a pretty stone or a marble

I made a small box for you and told you to keep your treasures.
That you were always looking for light,
for beauty in the earth, gold like trapped sun;
that I marveled at everything you made and kept.
That I've saved them all.

That, last summer, when you'd put on your new dress
I brought out the pearl you'd once found, shaped like a heart,
and said *Remember this?*

That I showed you the fields, full of green and gold,
always under the wind and said *This is your kingdom*,
that we tend and care and bring forth beauty and life
from the earth. *This is your land.*

iii

I regret that I let your father
carry you on his shoulders,
laughing like the sea breeze.
That he and I would stand, watching you sleep
while the moon slid in under the window like a ghost.
That I said you were an angel, a gift from the gods.

That I had loved you so much, so perfectly.
I thought I'd found what I was missing.
That you more than made up for what was lost.

That when you were a teenager, I let you sit in the dark
and read, so you were never afraid of the dark.
When your book was done you would often walk in the garden
at night, sometimes still tending the sleeping flowers,
or writing in your journal.

That I gave you the journal as soon as you could write,
and I told you to write. That I never read what you wrote
out of respect for you.

That I hadn't taught you to be afraid of the dark,
so you would always be comfortable and brave
wherever you were.

iv

Is it wrong of me to think that if you'd been afraid,
you would have come back to me?
Should I have raised a timid girl, a girl for whom the world was full
of demons, of poison?

I regret that I had ever wished
for a child at all, a girl;
that I dreamed.
That the day you became mine I knelt and prayed
and thanked the gods for you.

That I didn't offer to take your place.

v

Yes, all that, but mostly this:

That I remember.

Day of Reckoning

My mother doesn't want a headstone;
she wants to be cremated

and could I please scatter her ashes
somewhere in Lake Michigan.

My father wants to be returned to the land,
the earth—not in one place but many,

the way seeds disperse in the wind
hoping to find a place to grow. As if

I ever had a place to go,
a body to call home that wasn't a foraging—
as if I were not alone in the dark
watching the headlights of someone passing through

solitary in the quiet,
the moonlight bleeding through the window.

To the Neighbor's Young Daughter
who is Learning to Be Brave

Have you ever seen a thrust of wind
cut a tree branch to the quick,
leaving a bright wound open to the sky?

See what happens.

A crew comes to seal the branch,
staunch the bleeding.

The light fills.

A new shoot grows.

Someone takes a picture
of the tree's new shape and says
now it looks like my mother,
that time she stood at the beach,
arms wide out,
reaching for us
and the whole

universe out there,

waiting to be taken in.

Five Simple Dots of Light

My father is learning to text on his new smartphone;
his messages come through garbled and often unreadable,
like the old distant collect-call messages
when you had just three, maybe five seconds
to yell "Come pick me up!" before the operator's voice came on
and asked if they'd accept the call.

In my frustration, I pause and put my phone down
because my therapist says I need to isolate my emotions,
to stop and feel them, really feel them, so I can name them
and don't react so quickly.

But how can I name something so vague,
so indeterminate, so consuming
as watching your 70-year-old father struggle
with the easiest, smallest task?

My mother says nothing is ever just one thing.
This tiny set of letters and words I type
black on the screen like flocks of birds
scattered on the white winter sky
is not simply letters. It is pixels and light particles
that rotate and flicker as they catapult
through the wide invisible gasp of space
to land
—a stroke of pure luck, when you think about it—
as the speck that forms the dot
of the question mark in *How are you?*

The briefest reach of connection,
an impulse transmitted from the tips
of our fingers to the keyboard
moors us to place, makes possible
something meaningful and permanent,
if only for moments.

When I pick up the phone again, my father has sent
okay sweetheart, sleep well
and tries to send a heart, but it comes out
as five simple dots of light.

In the Red Room

Almost nothing has shadows:
the inundated colors, the thick lines
like full-rivered deltas. Pomegranate red

saturating the light, the way it is
in dreams: everything quivers, wholly alive—
flowers creeping on every surface,

tablecloth, wallpaper, even the woman
curled toward the vase keeps
rhythm, holds still black and white

near the open, wide window
where red doesn't reach;
her fingers buried in the vase,

her face expressionless, given over to vision—
memory pulls a scene from deep water,
wrings it out:

How red the pomegranate seeds
stained my hands, their bittersweet

essence on my tongue, the whiteness
of the plate

my father set out, his knife
slicing

what to give
and what

to discard, removing pith
with utter knowledge.

Self-Portrait as Persephone

There's the sand. And the wind carrying
clear sound, like the open mouth of the sea.

All of it rising, all at the same time, like myth:
a fish, a shell, a kiss—divine happening.

I remember how at 15
I wanted to be a muse: rising like myth

out of the green foam and beautiful, wondrous
as sea glass left behind on the shoreline—

a swallow, a burst, the shallow opening—
but a life is not a myth.

A life is a group of pits, a story of wandering
grief, following, becoming, returning, arriving.

Were it all a myth,
the wheat, the sun, the spring—

the open waving wind hitting the earth—
and the sea, the sea.

Poem with an Elephant

My son imagines families of animals who live with us.
Often it's a family of dogs or kittens, birds
(red parrots, specifically), rabbits, squirrels—but
today he reminds us of the elephant who lives
in my husband's jacket pocket.

Occasionally the elephant trumpets when we're waiting
in line at the grocery store or stuck in traffic.

Sometimes an elephant is a shadow.

Other times an elephant is a reminder of an old friend, a past
        wish that never came true;
                and sometimes an elephant is a metaphor.

                Sometimes an elephant makes a sound;
                        at times, silence sounds like an elephant.
Other times, it's sleeping, or playing at the park,
or vacuuming, or eating peanuts.
But not *real peanuts. Elephants don't really do that, Mom.*

Sometimes an elephant is a cough of grief.
        Other times, a ghost looks like a ghost, but is really an elephant.

Often the elephant is quiet, but my son is wise enough
to know that doesn't mean the elephant is gone.

        Sometimes an elephant looks like a giant when it is just a dream.
Once in a while an elephant is not an absence.

Sometimes the wind over the lake sounds like an elephant
        but really it is just the heaviness of the sound of me missing you.

Girl Talk

Over lunch my friend says,
Maybe I just need a good divorce so I can lose this weight.

I say *No, no*--
but I know what she means.

It's hard to lose weight when you have children
and dogs and families and jobs—

and there's the preschool science project.
And spirit day—the *red* shirt, not the *blue* one!

And the meeting with the boss who just doesn't understand
why you're never at the coffee hour after 2:30 pm.

Then there's always the question of dinner—takeout, these days—
because who has time to cook
(especially with kids who won't eat it anyway).

After lunch, she says she thinks she wants to get lap band surgery
and *do you think I should*

I say *I will support whatever decision you make*

And she says But would you

I say no
but what I mean is, I want the easy way out, but I won't do it.

I say *You can't live without tacos*
and what I really mean is,
I want to keep doing what I already do, without guilt–honestly,
what I'm tired of is all this guilt.

When she says *Nah I don't think I'm ready for that*
what she means is she's tired, too,
so I tell her she looks cute in her new workout clothes.

Sometimes Demeter Wishes...

Sometimes I wish I'd never had a child
and I could go on without making meaning
of everything, seeing my disembodied love
everywhere—

not hearts and hands and bodies
reaching for each other.

Can we learn what it is
to love beyond the seasons?

Today the sun is a gas in the sky.
Its smear varnishes the tops of trees.
Withered leaves cling to the oaks.
Pines slope, lean in toward the clean sun,
its gray grief slowly leeching from the sky.

Blackbird, Butterfly, Robin

When my mother said
she'd never seen
a red-winged blackbird,
she meant at her age she had seen most
of what she was going to see,

and isn't it incredible to know
there's still a whole lot of surprise left
in the world—

like how when I saw a butterfly
and a robin fly at the same time
in a single patch of air last summer

I thought, *this is what it's like to be loved*
and when I say *loved*

I mean you touched me
and it was the first time I've ever
felt like flying.

Sometimes Love Looks Just Like a Field

I see it everywhere, its golden arms stretching
to hold the earth and all its color.

I used to stand at its hem and gaze
when I wanted to feel big and small at the same time:

big, towering over flowers, crushing clover leaves,
my footprints forming paths as if the world
were only mine to shape;

small atop a bulge, everything else beyond
like the spread of the sea, and me
a pawn in the wind, baffled at the vast
roll under all that hefty light.

There I am—a little girl running through the golden stalks,
high grass tangled in my hair.
The busy pines jut out to eavesdrop.
There's nothing else but my tiny hand.

At the edge, my father—tall and strong as a tree—
will carry me home on his shoulders
when the sting comes and I swell
with light and toxins.

Self-Portrait Where My Mother is a Nun
and I'm a Good Daughter

In all the photos, I'm a dimpled smiling child;
in the world behind them I'm running away,
coming back only to reassure myself
that my mother is still there.

Now I'm older than she was then and much less sure
where she will be if I run to her:
will she still hold her arms out for my embrace,
or would it startle her, grown unused to the tumble
of a young child's unruly arrival?

Her devotion was legendary, like Demeter's—
whose despair ravaged the earth
until her beloved daughter was returned, but

what happens when the daughter
does not run back to her mother?

My therapist reminds me
it was Demeter's bargaining with her brother
that returned Persephone to the world.

What might the story have been
if Persephone had chosen to stay?

Did you know, I tell my therapist today, *in high school
my mother wanted to be a nun?*
I don't know if she ever understood why,
but it makes sense to me.

I worry about how we can live together
if she becomes ill.

I lack the patience and devotion.

But who will remain when water floods the earth?

Who—when everything else is washed away—
will cloak herself in wimple and robes,
silent as the prayers rattling voiceless throats,
and move as quickly as fingers along the beads?

The Rabbit

This morning I saw a dead baby rabbit
in the backyard, flies swirling around its small body,
soft with death. Yesterday I had seen it moving,
wounded, with the slow quiet of inevitability.

As I wrestled the carcass onto the shovel,
I thought of its mother, somewhere invisible,
wondering if she were watching me try to care
for her dead offspring. I could see how I must look to her,

a bent awkward figure in the corner of the yard,
wielding the shovel's once sky-blue tooth,
now worn gray and white from years of scraping
ice and heaving snow, accustomed
to dragging things from one place to another.

When I finally tied the loose ends of the plastic bag
and placed it in the garbage can, I saw a gull
soar in the wide sky. What was it looking for?
I watched it pass, watched the sky
begin to fill with clouds.

Later, I lie awake in my son's bed.
The light behind the clouds flashes blue
with late-summer storms, thunder
hurtling somewhere above like the clatter
and thump of my son's toy instruments
when he plays marching band.

I think of the mother rabbit once again,
how tonight she will huddle underground
or behind a bush, away from the hard rain.
I watch how the storm flares in the little
triangle between the blinds and the window,
while my son settles slowly in to sleep
like a restless pond.

Paradise

Our Bird of Paradise is suffering
from some kind of fungus or mold.
Its long green neck seems faded to sallow gray
in places, like an old bruise.
Yet today it blooms, its sharp
flowers still an offering.

When I pull up to the house I can see it
against the front window
pressed against the glass
the way my grandmother stood at her porch window

waving goodbye to us,
back-lit always by shallow lamplight
until we were out of view.

SUMMER

In the Kingdom of Light

[Hades sits, stage right]

Each morning I wake to the stale hollow
sound of death.
Even when I turn out the light,
it hums like a sea of crickets beneath my feet.

> *[Persephone, stage left, stands in front of a mirror
> on a vanity.]*
>
> Once I believed that if I swallowed
> my fear, it would go away.
> But what was it you said?
> *[she turns toward a bed, as if a person sat there]*
>
> *You cannot find peace by avoiding darkness?*

The scent of death seeps into my skin
so deep even fire cannot burn it off.

> I swallowed those seeds.
> I was so hungry.
>
> Never in my life had I felt such hunger:
> its heavy branches spread through me
> and I didn't know if I would ever be free
> from their clutching.

[shaking head]
Sometimes you have to smoke things out.
Sometimes you have to kill something to see it up close.

[Hades stands and walks toward center stage]

Your pale body, a world inside a world within itself,
sings of the white poplar I cannot shake, the white
poplar of my memory holding court in its kingdom of light.

[*Persephone walks to the bed, lies down*]

I didn't know if I could really believe
that to swallow anything
would bind me to history and my fate,
good daughter that I am.

We love bodies that remind us of other bodies,

[*as if overcome, Persephone bolts upright,
walks to center stage as if to face Hades*]

songs that remind us of other songs.

Now—I stand on the only anchor between realms.

[*Hades returns to seat, mimes turning on lamp*]

In darkness, light is a blessing.
Against its silhouette, almost anything is possible.

Almost anything is possible.

When we get what we hope for, it
tastes good.
Then it becomes an old dress we try on
to see how the mirror
ages.

[*Hades gestures towards center stage to Persephone,
whom he can't see*]

I know how they'll tell the story—
that you shrank from me, from my touch,
on the couch—
but I knew how hungry you were.

[*Persephone: bows head*] How hungry I was.

What if joy happens by another name?

What if joy happens by another name?
All I could offer you were those seeds.
I didn't know if you would take them.

[*Persephone looks up, turns towards audience*]
If, when it grows, I take it, it moves like fog,
like something with feathers.

[*Hades, pleading, accusatory*]
Do you think I'm the one who poisoned the world?
One cannot stop a heart from breaking

One cannot stop a heart from breaking,
but you can't take it with you
into the next life,
or the one after that.

[*Hades points toward audience*]
What do you know of the next life or of death?

Let me tell you: there is no savior among the raucous world,
nor beneath.

[*Hades and Persephone turn, simultaneously, to face each other*]:

Does nothing in this wild world forgive?

Persephone, Her First Summer Back Home

I step out into summer air full of wet and heat.

In the garden, the small cucumber,
pendulous on its great spray of yellow and green vines,
is now three times larger than two days ago.

This has already happened, and is happening.

Everything in my field of vision opens, and is opening.

The light splits into rods as long as trees.
The air fills.

Birds soar and continue soaring.

I think of you and the dark width that is your hands,
how it holds my heart like
the stakes my mother plunged into the earth,
into the garden that leans into its own undoing.

The Thing You Thought You Wanted

We saw a snake skin lying
in the grass outside the garage,
almost fully intact, and shaded in places
with traces of its former scales.
The snake had left, entering the world
in its new skin the way a storm creeps up
to fill the day, the way when I asked you
if you had seen the snake
you said you didn't find anything,
it had already passed,
its deflated shape on the warm July lawn.

The Deepest Images of Our Universe are Here on Earth

This photograph shows an area of space
that would be the size of a grain of sand held at arm's length
to a person standing on Earth, depicting a galaxy cluster
4.6 billion light-years away.

This photograph shows what a scrap
of the universe looked like billions of years ago.
This photograph shows the invisible dreams
of people who spent their days making this technology
so someday we could say
This photograph shows what we didn't, couldn't see,
what we didn't know we didn't know.
This photograph looks like a beach of black
sand at night & the shells lit up by bioluminescence. Or maybe
this photograph looks like something else.

In the face of such enormity & perfection, do we have words?
Can we imagine what it is like to be without
the palm of gravity gently pressing us into our forms?

Valerie asks if I've seen the photos & says
There must be life out there—

I respond we cannot be the only
beings thrusting heartbeats from perilous, ephemeral
cages of our anxious chests into the emptiness.
Even the rain has a soul. See it? That drop which just shattered
on the hot July sidewalk looks like a galaxy,
with planets & stars & something whole, thick,
flush at the bitter center.

In the Watermelon Fields of Kansas

The melons sleep like planets in the heavy morning.
Sometimes you'd find half-eaten carcasses clinging to their vines,
entrails spilled on the sandy soil, leaves green and oblivious
as ever, still threading life into empty wounds. Or a ragged white gash
from a rough pocket knife that sheared the vine into a phantom limb:
a premature rescue by someone who hadn't scanned the prairie's
prim horizon for the gray breath of storm, who hadn't rushed
out at the first sign to rescue their bulging, mottled bellies
from piercing hail, from burning in the mouth of the sun.
The heirloom watermelons—named *Moon and Stars* for the yellow galaxy
on their humped backs—still sing on the tongue.
Those who rescue are invisible. Even now, you hold one out
in front of you as if to say *here is the world made new and sweet.*

Poem with Husband and Turtle

My husband told me he helped a turtle cross the road this morning.
I asked *Are you supposed to do that?*

Because the world is often in need of explanation.

Sometimes we need permission for kindness.

Tikkun olam is a funny thing—
sometimes repairing the world is a need so ocean-like
we can't get around it.

Sometimes it feels monstrous and holy,
and other times I don't even know who or what it is,
or how it holds itself along my body.

Sometimes it is invisible, often small
and insignificant, like the scent of a fresh peach.

Other times, it is unwieldy and unyielding,
unexplainable but pulsing
with the blood of its own existence

just entirely, wholly there.

Shouldn't we let things that are wholly what they are
be what they are?

He replies, *it could have been killed by a car.*
So I carried it across, in the direction it was going, and waited for it.

What happened then? I asked.

It waited for me to get out of the way,
and then kept going.

The thought of you singing

imperfect
in the shallow burnished light,
opens what is also imperfect and true in me.

Voices often come from places we cannot see:
humming of tree frogs green and hollow,
joyful in their song.

Listen to them in this cursive quiet.
Their constant murmur hems the night,
mends it back into place.

Hades Advises Demeter

Let the fruit of my labor linger
in your lungs like fog
after a long wet week.

Let the minerals, the ore in the earth
bloom to fire, to ash and sediment,
to line the rivers we drink from.
Step in to know what it is we become.

You can know only what the skin stores.

All else melts, becomes the thirst of roots,
seeds, haunted sky.

Let clouds bleed to feed
the earth, fill the river.

Where there are ghosts
there was life.

To love anything is to bear
witness, shadow our hearts.

Let our light
love what it wants,
darken what it needs.

Persephone to Hades, Late August

You want to know how I'm doing.
You want to know if I miss our life.

Everywhere I go I can smell the river.
I hear it, too.

I'm always thinking of things to say to you.
About summer. About how the light keeps falling
over everything, very like a river.
So much of my life is rivers now.
I see them everywhere.
In the garden.
In the curve of flower petals.
How the wind, too, is a river—
how it rustles along trees, carving space
between trunks and branches.

I have written and unwritten
many notes. Nothing sticks.
What to say to her, to you,
about any of this?

If I say I forgive you—if I forgive you—
then does the part of me that wants something from you,
that wants you—
does that mean a part of me has died?

What then?

2,300 Friday Nights

The X-ray of my jaw gapes before me.
Sitting in the dentist's chair I realize
you never see your own skeleton—

you only ever get a model: a dark, blurry
picture, a faded fragment, as if one easily
stands in for the other.

Tomorrow, I will call the bank.
I want a new mortgage:
30 more unbroken years
and many more meadows
drenched in crocus light and wayward winds
crowned by glistening city lights full
of stars and a briny moon.

It turns out that at any given moment
we can see at most 3,000 stars.
Maybe one burns clear like the best-cut diamond
for every Friday night I have left.

Hades, Summer Solstice

Afternoon. Pigeons and crows, other dark birds
perch on gray wires, patient,
as undemanding as the long summer light.

There are things we recognize only
with closed throat,
eyes shuttered like winter.

I remember nighttime in the blackest part of the year,
dark but for the cold blue stars
holding heavy their dots of solid light.

I remember the gesture of my body
and your eyes, how they anticipated
my curve toward you
in my own orbit,
how I retreated in wide black safety, full
of the knowledge that once you let something go,
it never returns the way it came.

After Death

On the day after my friend's father died,
we walked by the lake, almost touching,
our bodies remembering closeness, the way trees
record ecological events in their rings. He watched
a white sailboat glide into harbor. I watched his hands
fall to his sides. A shard of beach glass, green as olives,
glistened in the water. It felt heavier than it should
as I held it, as if pulled by an anchor.

Above, the gulls circled silently. When he turned back toward me,
I told him how in some cemeteries now your body can become a tree,
how when you're buried, I think, somehow your heart lives on.
We walked and saw a dead lake trout, its skin still waterlogged,
head hinged open after something had eaten it, perhaps where the soul
had left the body. I told him, *Did you know that before a female octopus dies,*
she stops eating and lets her body wither? She often shreds her skin,
eats the tips of her own tentacles, tears herself to pieces.

Last year in the same spot, we stopped to look
at the large dead pike lying in a perfect frozen comma against the ragged shore,
its glossy black skin shimmering. Adults paused
their strolling to gaze at it; children quietly knelt over it, whispering
to each other and poking it with sticks as if to rouse it—
as if the sudden nudge would jolt it out of its repose.

A heart attack, he said. I was at the hospital all night,
but his body was too old, too weak, to take the shock.

I wonder if that's what happened to the octopus in New Zealand
who escaped its tank; shimmying through a small gap
and down through pipes into the open bay.
The octopus escaped not out of boredom or unhappiness
but the feeling, within the core of its cells, that life had been so full
and large it could not contain even its flexible form.

The Field

The first thing I ever loved was a field—
tall grass stained by sun, drenched with flowers, gold
everywhere. I wanted to rub it on my body
so my skin would glow.

My mother says the first thing I loved was the ocean.

> *I would put your feet in and then you were out,*
> *coasting over the waves, too far,*
> *as if you wanted to drink it, swim*
> *all the way to the horizon.*

I did.

I wanted it to engulf me, to swallow its translucent cold,
have it grow and bloom within me, to become it,
full and deep and wider than what I could see, could know.

Can we love before we know we are an I?

Today I see the slow, wide ribbons of grass swollen
with crops and light, and it is as if I am looking at the sea,
as if the two blur in God's pentimento.
And farther than the eye's line, fields flood like water
right up to all the edges, tractors and silos motionless,
the slow trundle of terrain
like the quiet water before waves stretch
and hurl themselves to shore,
earth become water, water become earth.

At the lip of a spade, life spills out
of the earth like a spring.

I have gathered up its bounty and rolled it into seeds.
I have sown my hair through the earth

and let it dance on the wind like spores,
doused my feet in grass.

I have felt the water and the light
baptize my skin.
I have taken within my body
the salt from the water,
the minerals from the earth,
the elements of light.

Standing before this gilded field,
I know that if it opens, if
I drown in its thick light,
I will be ready.

Daily Work

For one whole beautiful day,
bees throng our poppies,
doting on their delicate silk petals.

With the bees come robins and finches,
sleepy ladybugs, admiring eyes,
the gentle glossy wind.
The warm sun, heavy and full
above everything.

Love is an intransitive verb

My friend Martin says he's been thinking about the flag
and how he's come to understand it is not
just an empty symbol. What he loves about it,
he says, is that it can represent all of us, what
the promise of America could be.
He wears it on his sleeve like the badge
of the patron saint of lost causes. We all want
to help one another. I've been thinking about him
thinking about the flag. I've been thinking I want
to be a person who loves the flag and loves thinking
about America. I want to love so much of this misshapen
and misbegotten abundance, the tattered bug-ridden
underbelly: rats in the subway. Garbage dumps
and rivers swollen with bacteria. The plastic and refuse
that washes up on beaches as dunnage, shell-hash.
The bacteria that invaded my grandfather's blood,
turning it septic; my mother's uterine metastasis,
threatening my own genes like a covenant.
I want to love the politicians, the people who want
to vacuum carbon emissions out of the air.
The billionaires and celebrities who jet off to space
instead of solving world hunger or poverty.
It is easy to love when everything is beautiful.
I want to be a person who can love others
as easily as breathing: the way the sun
embraces the world and highlights its imperfections.
Here's a cracked abandoned cement wall. Here's
the withered ancient ivy snaking up its shabby back.
Here's where the thick vines ruin the view of the window, outline
the jagged stained glass so you can't see the world
outside anymore. Here's where ivy grew.

Stocking the Lagoon

The dark lagoon is velvet with blackbirds.
After thaw, people—mostly children—fish
with makeshift poles from the muddy water,
lines rippling like echoes the weight
of gravity's thick palm on the body.

Swallows and ducks, gulls and geese,
even the blackbirds have come to expect this regular
pinch at the surface, the cast and release
of debris and insect, fish-brine and glint of reel.

Children and hungry birds
do not know that fish are thrust
into this shallow fen, a quivering mass of light
that shimmers and will soon dissolve.

Dream (Persephone)

Ever since I was a girl
(so much of me is nothing;
loneliness taps always at my window)

I've had a dream
where in a clearing
under a huge gold tent of light
I saw the man I would marry.
All I could look at were his hands.

They were white as new lambs
and clean; they looked
like they could soften death,
smooth its ridges on the body.

Even when he finally wrapped his arms around me
to carry me over a dark threshold,
I didn't notice
because I was looking at his hands and
the shape they made of my destiny.

Entering the World Again

The Mexican food truck is a darker blue this year
and now festooned with icicle lights, because it's festive,
and this is a festive occasion. So far, three black dogs,
two puppies, four kids screaming, and two red wagons.

>The playground is an amoeba of children and motion.
>Parents pitch lawn tents and camping chairs
>and on the side of the hill, squares of heirloom quilts,
>old blankets, coolers, and more beer.

There are screams and cicadas, the skid of scooter tires,
and the gulp-zap! of tennis balls on the courts across the street.
Beyond, the beer tent and beyond that the bandshell
and beyond that the jagged tree tops crest the sky,
holding vigil.

>When the band starts its first chords, dusk does too
>and the whole mess of everything we are seems
>to shimmer and stop, shimmer and stop—
>like old home movies with bright and blurry light.

We are here, now. We do not know what we want
except to be here, but we are here and it is July
and we are ready.

>And when a plane flies overhead,
>it can probably see us too, all of us here,
>under this patch of the sun,
>before it lands, before its passengers pour out
>and enter the world again.

Parachuters

Twice I thought they were birds—
the sky today is full of them, bursting
into precise formations on their way south.

Then I spied an arm, a leg, the spangle of a rainbow
parachute, the careful sideways descent,
and I thought: I know what it's like to want
to soar, to be for a moment untethered from loss.

Summer ends, day by day, long moment by long moment.
We do not see its shape until it has passed.

FALL

Tether

Tall silhouettes of cornstalks, for now still green,
stand rigid in the swollen light.
Milkweed pods begin to form on their thin stems.
Air rings with memory
as it remains forever afternoon.

I drive the roads we drove
just to be out in the space of the world.
We'd drive into weather, headlong
into the hysterical snow swirling,
flailing to secure itself to something.

Under wide clouds I gather seeds from the wind,
send them back to the earth,
remember how in the curve of your palm
things kept warm.

Now the wind strokes the grass.
The faded crops howl to be cut,
to lie down and rest. Stay small.

Snow will come to drape their shriveled limbs,
but the roots, deep below the frozen earth,
linger, anchor what remains.

Persephone on Fate

i.

He said if you stand here you can watch the ferry come in.

The river was still as glass, and black.
I put my hand in to see if the water rippled.

Instead I saw my shape—clearer than in life, and brighter.

Without shadows, things look different.

When the ferry comes, not even the water moves.

ii.

He could have been my father.
He could have been my teacher.
Was he my husband? Was he a savior?

I could have been his disciple.

None of that matters now.

Does the truth survive a story?
Does life survive the truth?

iii.

The story of my unbecoming goes like this:

his hand, full of seeds, wanted to give.
Mine, empty of desire, wanted to take.

And then we turned into our fate.

Isn't that how it goes?
Doesn't everything end in words?

Not ashes to ashes, dust to dust,
but life into words.

We are spun. We are storied.
Reflections on an unrippled river.
Unchanged, myth on the page.

After Demeter's therapist tells her to find 5 things she can see to cope with her anger and grief

I see the mountain-blue mist of barren trees
trimming the horizon.

The haunted bales of hay loll
eerie on the hips of the hills.

The ochre fields move in the wind like the sea.

The gulls, white, as if fashioned from paper,
gather in long empty windrows.

The red tractor, its maw open, waits.

Listen, I know what heartbreak is—
I had my ways: I mourned

a dead carcass licked clean by predators
and lying in a green lush lush, green field.

I built fires from stones; planted seeds
where before none could grow.

I have set the table for two
and then gone on a picnic alone.

This is different.

That is my sun bleeding over the hills.

This is my land mowed to the quick and seething.

Erev Rosh Hashanah

The grass is a chorus of crickets
under the dappled late-morning sky.

The houses on 64th and Marion, trimmed
with their singing green lawns and ancient trees

steep in the heavy air.
The light has not yet turned, not yet—

those somnolent elms reach skyward and earthward,
stretch for meaning in both directions.

Yom Kippur

I watch the garden slowly die.

The air tapers, leaves almost ready to fall.

Evening's dampness darkens before it spreads.

We have waited for the late tomatoes,
scarlet, bulbous, brooding
until we pull them from their vines.

Whatever comes, comes slowly.

Only the fox appears suddenly.

What have we given this season?

What have we filled
with breath and light?

God Loves You '22

(after Erika Meitner)

declares the billboard on my commute
this morning, towering over the ragtag surf
of cars and highway, everyone busy on their way
to work or school, the lives we live outside our homes
in a holy testament to our love for America and capitalism.
I tell a colleague it reminds me of her
and she says *I just assume everything is Packers now*
since she's just moved to Wisconsin,
our worship of balloon-men in spandex pants and over-blown
padding and a shiny helmet, our paean to Sunday
and togetherness and aggression, watching grown men
fight and tumble again and again, their bodies worn
temples to injury and strife. So much aggression
leaves invisible scars. So many of my friends tell me
their husbands of 10-15-20-25 years have snapped—
they are angry. They have aggression they don't know
what to do with, didn't know they had. They don't even call
it aggression. They call it *stress at work*. Jealousy.
They call it falling in love with another person. Another friend told me
she loved the Beatles *Get Back* documentary
but *I think they are all unmoored.*
I pass under the bridge where a few years ago
several people tried to jump into oncoming traffic—
a sign plastered over the narrow railing
in blue Sharpie THANKS FOR EVERYTHING, GOODBYE.
On erev Rosh Hashana my mother-in-law asks her brother
if he's eaten his apples and honey.
She gets up from the table to remind everyone
to eat their apples dipped in honey, take in
a morsel sweetened by the viscous liquid
of nectar and enzymes, made and stored by bees
for eating in times of scarcity. My mother-in-law truly believes
in this ritual. I don't believe in anything. I'm uncomfortable
with even the notion of God except when it's maybe

convenient. But aren't we all unmoored, road-warriors,
witnesses to this jumbled landscape of televangelism
and testament and testimony?—*God loves us*
even when we don't love him. When my mother-in-law returns
I take an apple slice and pour the honey over
and it drips onto my shirt, a sticky blemish
I don't notice until today while I'm walking in
to work, the early morning light full now, and open.

Conchology

Once I met a man who carried a mussel shell in his pocket.
His specialty was conchology—the study of mollusk shells.
He loved their black oval arches mottled with the afterimage
of barnacles and sinews; he admired the white gloss glazing their undersides
the way the moonlight lines the sea. He had no use for the scar
of teeth, the bite of sweat, for guts hidden only by the thin grease
of skin and smile or even the heavy-duty bulk of a heart—
just the idea of a shell, a clean polished mass clinging to rocks by the thinnest
of threads. Don't you want to be strong? he asked. *Don't you want
a firm, rigid shell holding you in?*

Etrog

The same day I learned that the AI voice in my car can say *fuck*,
I also learned that I'd forgotten it was erev Yom Kippur,

and also the anniversary of my grandfather's death
more than 15 years ago, where in the temple for the service

the rabbi compared him to the etrog,
the now-sacred citrus fruit only grown in Israel for Sukkot;

which is also the same day I realized there's no one alive
to settle the debate about whether my great-grandmother's name

was Molly or Rebecca; and no one is alive whom I can ask
about whether my grandmother pureed the sauce for the meatballs,

or whom she loved before she loved my grandfather
and whether she really wanted a daughter

or how many hours it really takes to make the brisket,
and honestly—*honestly*—what was the secret ingredient in the cookies;

and no one is alive whom I can ask what the light
looked like in the dark *shtetl* evenings or how it felt

to see the rows and rows of the *etrogs*
quietly gleaming in the morning when the market opened.

Farginen

This morning I read *A civilian is shot in a police station*
& multiple news outlets repeat the ambiguous summary
initially released by the Chicago Police Department,
making it unclear who *shot* who.

I want to correct this to *whom*, because grammar
is how I order the world, slide the unruly tongue-slips
into their places for comfort—but I don't. I'm practicing
kindness, or whatever it is we call restraint these days.
I am trying to be a better person, though my bullshit
reserves are running on the fumes of fumes
because I keep thinking of how nothing (language-wise
or otherwise) is getting any better. Right now I'm thinking
of my late grandmother who cried "No one has any compassion
anymore!" at every news story. I wonder what she'd say now
when almost every day we wake up to another shooting
or a new war zone in the place they buried Rabbi Nachman
of Breslov or the fact that over 1 million people have died
from COVID-19. The hurricanes are getting bigger, stronger.
I don't think it is compassion she would mourn
in all this suffering. We know how to suffer, to recognize
an/other's suffering. We have even adopted
Schadenfreude because we delight in our prayers
for those waiting for hurricanes to strike, to blow barren & empty
their homes, windsweep entire communities from the map
like topographies seen from space. Compassion has gone astray.

Today on the second day of Rosh Hashanah I'm reminded
of the word in Yiddish, *farginen*, that means genuine pride
& joy in an/other's success. Look—it's no longer
springtime & so everything is starting to die. But last night
a cottontail came back to our yard
after many weeks & found the wilting tomato plants
in the garden. I watched it nibble a lone
forgotten tomato before it noticed me, before its departure
became a swift blur of white motion.

All Hallows

We're in the deep V of autumn now,
and my son has three Halloween costumes
that he likes to wear to breakfast,
after which he will change into the other and back again.
He slips into these identities—pirate, Spider-man, Captain America—
as easily as the moon slips among hers.

Even the swim instructor slides in and out of Spanish
like a salmon twisting in a burst of river.
Fabian. Diego. Sophia. Michael, he calls, windmilling his arm
above his head as the children learn their bodies
in the water, how it changes the way they move,
how easy to mistake their buoyancy for a new skin,
a new form.

On the way home from swim class,
we watch the breeze gather the leaves to piles,
the trees bare against a smoke-white sky
that drapes, as my son points out,
like the cobwebs strung for decoration
on some houses and bushes.

Alongside the road, I notice a deer carcass
worn, speeding tire after speeding tire,
to a flat mess of entrails and dirt,
clumps of fur still stuck to what remains
of bones and sinews.

Only the stiff head stares forward.
Even at speed I see how straight its stare,
how quiet it seems in its death, how ready.
After a week of rain and cool weather,
its head never falls, never wavers,
even as we rush by.

Ritual

At Thanksgiving, I always think of my aunts
who washed the dishes after dinner,
a sort of dance like a flock of birds on the snow—

one moves here, another tosses a dishtowel there,
one side-steps a dog. Then what to do about dessert:
who's setting out the coffee; which one has cleaned the forks.

Where are the goddamned napkins?
This year, a cousin brought her new boyfriend
and could it be? No. Not yet.

The autumn light dims in the sky
as if bronzed. Somewhere, we are playing house,
playing at living. Someone yells out, *Pie! Dessert!*

Suddenly there is a scrum of children, forks poised,
laughing. Then my mother, dish towel still in hand,
steps aside.

What did we know then of the comfort
of ritual and its hidden stains?

An Old White Door

Tracy has canceled all her plans and says
The kids and I have Covid and I have a dead dog
so if anyone has a problem with that, they can go to Hell.

At the cemetery, there's a grave decorated with toys.

My father refuses to speak ill of the dead.

Jews plant trees, bring casseroles and sit for seven days with their mourning.
Some tell stories, say prayers and light candles. I focus on my smile

in the picture from Christmas Eve, 1984, instead of the fact
that it was taken while my mother miscarried my sister's twin.
Perhaps that's why my sister fills the house with people, names her daughter

after her dead friend. I write to Valerie, *Isn't grief just love leaving the body?*

My husband and I cleaned out his grandmother's apartment, hung her art
on our living room walls. We named a drawer in the kitchen after her
because it held the El-Al airlines spoon she used to feed her grandchildren.

My aunt got a new dog the same weekend hers died
because she couldn't stand the quiet.
A friend goes to the spa after taking her mother to hospice.

The cake I baked last month for my neighbor
whose father died suddenly at 64 was baked
in my grandmother's cake pans.

My mother now regularly sends me old photos. I think it's because she knows
whatever is left in their house when they die, we will have to clean up.
Because she knows we know someday she is going to die.

Today on my walk I saw a red chair and an old white door on the sidewalk.
The chair was small enough to be a child's or maybe a place
to sit to remove your shoes.

I stopped and thought, you could use the door to make a table or a bench
or divide a room or a life raft when everything floods
and you need something to hang on to.

pomegranate/seeded apple/beginnings

ancient fruit/of the dead/the fertile crescent
  birthed civilizations/fertile fruits of the land/its seeds
    like blood/like the blood of the women who bring forth
At Rosh Hashanah/we eat its bloody flesh/new beginning New Year/
    open like a wound/a world/of bloody teeth
Jews say when you kill a man you kill a world/ you extinguish
  his children and his children's children/ when a woman
    is in the womb/she has all the eggs she will ever have/imagine
    civilizations/6 million Jews died in the camps/
when my father first showed me a pomegranate
  he let me hold the seeds in my hands/
    I put one in my mouth and sucked the fruit
my lips and tongue and hands stained/
  with their juice/a bloody covenant
    /like Persephone's
her bloody covenant: she ate/these seeds/of life and death/
  to seal her fate/to mark her queen/of the dead
    born of life/within her/ both worlds/
within me within us worlds upon worlds
    each seed a world/its promise continuance/ I used to think
    altruism/now I know
    even seeds are selfish/one singular purpose: to grow (only) into itself
    its beauty /its undoing/its whole life
  for propagation/to nourish its/self
and when we eat the seeds/we continue/what we eat we are
  what seeds we eat leave us/empty/
    of promise /now/
  their whole world's inside of us/to begin
    again its cycle/its birth/
  its death

NOTES

"Paradise" includes a line by Etel Adnan found in an email exchange published soon after Adnan's death. The line reads: "Paradise doesn't have to be beautiful. It just has to make us happy."

Tikkun Olam, literally "repair the world," derives from Hebrew; and it refers to the pursuit of social justice inherent in Judaism.

Erev, literally "evening," is the day before a Jewish holiday. Since Jewish holidays begin the day before at sundown, it's often common to wish someone "erev Rosh Hashonah" and some services—particularly during the High Holy days—take place on these evenings.

Rosh Hashanah: Jewish New Year; usually in September.

Yom Kippur: Day of Atonement, 8 days after Rosh Hashonah.

Farginen: Yiddish for "wholeheartedly celebrating or taking joy in the success of others"; it's the opposite of "schadenfreude."

"In the Red Room" uses Henri Matisse's *The Dessert (Harmony in Red)*, more commonly known as *The Red Room* as its ekphrasis.

"The Deepest Images of Our Universe are Here on Earth" refers to, and takes inspiration from, the July 2022 photograph released by NASA's James Webb telescope of galaxy cluster SMACS 0723. Dubbed "First Deep Field", the photograph refers to the "deepest and sharpest infrared image of the distant universe to date."

ACKNOWLEDGMENTS

The following poems have been published (sometimes in different form) in these journals:

"Hanukkah Dinosaur" and "Love is an intransitive Verb," *Rattle*

"How to Survive the Winter" and "Tether," *Feed*

"Mistletoe," *Parentheses*

"Clothesline," *SWWIM Miami*

"Demeter Unbound," *CP Quarterly*

"If He Had Offered Her His Heart" and "In the Kingdom of Light," *Birdcoat Quarterly*

"Givens," *Orange Blossom Review*

"Lost Cause," "The Watermelon Fields of Kansas," and "2300 Friday Nights," *Sledgehammer Review*

"Persephone's Lament, Early Spring," *The West*

"Day of Reckoning," *Rust & Moth*

"Learning to Be Brave (To the Neighbors' Young Daughter)," "Poem with Husband and Turtle," "Yom Kippur," and "pomegranate/seeded apple/beginnings," *Minyan Magazine*

"The Thing You Thought You Wanted," *Door is a Jar*

"Entering (the world again)," *Kissing Dynamite*

"Conchology," *Neologism*

I've never been a person who likes endings, partly because endings signal change. Though I have come to accept changes as a necessary and fruitful part of life, endings are still difficult for me. Finishing a project like this proved no different. What's more difficult now is finding words to express my gratitude and amazement at the folks around me, who continue—without end—to lift me up, carry me forward, and encourage me no matter what I'm doing.

First, the entire team at Cornerstone: all of you are incredible. Because of Dr. Ross Tangedal and his extraordinary vision, books like this get to live in the world, better than their authors could ever imagine. Thank you all for your attention, expertise, questions, vision, patience, commitment, and so much more. I'm honored, awed, incredibly grateful. This book would not be what it is if not for you.

Second, Kathleen Dale, as always, has read every single word more times than we can count, and it is of course this attention that's the gift. If not for your probing question about how Persephone would respond to her mother's feelings, I would not have written this book. Thank you for always asking the questions I need to move further. Thank you for your incredibly keen ability to see the poems, their potential. Thank you for patience.

To Allison Adair, Dr. Jenna Goldsmith, and Heathen Derr: your reviews continue to awe me in their generosity. The honor is entirely mine to have such fine writers, feminists, and poetry citizens to blurb this collection. Thank you, beyond words, for your kindness and attention.

No poet gets anywhere without readers, and I'm honored to have the best: Dr. Elizabeth Johnston and Jared Beloff, who each possess an unmatched commitment to the integrity of a poem; and whose keen eyes never fail to notice something I do not. Thank you for your patience, your time, your honesty. (And, in Jared's case, this amazing title!) Other such invaluable readers include Molly Sides, Martin Quirk, and Stuart Moulthrop. You all amaze me, every day.

I'd also like to publicly thank the following people who continue to show up for me even when I do not deserve it: Gabby Bachhuber, Kelly Baran, Valerie Blair, Allison Castillo, Ori Fienberg, Brett Griffiths, Becky and Dan Hansen, Derrick Harriell, Tracy Kruse, Liana Odrcic, Sheila Patel, Alexis Whyte, Lisa Woodall, and Kevin Wozniak. Thank you all for being the incredible folks you are.

Special and continued thanks to Alexis Whyte for her beautiful artwork adorning the cover—when I was asked for cover ideas, you're the first person I thought of to design it because of your talent, and it has surpassed my expectations.

To the women who have come before me and who come after, I see you. I hear you. I notice how you've been able to shape my life, even when you didn't have to. To Dr. Catherine Golden and Dr. Susan Kress, I thank you for your continued mentorship. Thanks for showing me the way all those years ago. I wouldn't be the writer, scholar, teacher, or poet I am without you.

But even with such an incredible team of incredible folks, I couldn't do what I do if not for my husband, Brad Houston; my son Gabriel; my sister, Audrey Etlinger; and my parents, Ron and Kathy Etlinger. You make whatever is good in my life possible, and it isn't easy. My love for you is boundless, endless, unwavering. Thank you. At the end of the day, there's nowhere I'd rather be.

SARAH A. ETLINGER is an English professor who lives in Milwaukee, Wisconsin, with her family. A two-time Pushcart and Best of the Net nominee, she is the author of three books: *Never One for Promises* (2018), *Little Human Things* (2020), and *The Weather Gods* (2023). Recent work has been nominated for inclusion in *Best Spiritual Writing* and has appeared in *Rattle, Rust & Moth, Minyan Magazine* (where she was Featured Poet), and *SWWIM Miami,* among many others.